# A GUIDE TO
# Christian Prayer and Fasting

*So then with the mind I myself serve the law of God; but with the flesh the law of sin.*

— ROMANS 7:25

## ANGELO E. QUINLAN

**New Harvest Time**
PUBLICATIONS

Published by New Harvest Time Publications

Copyright © 2017 Angelo E. Quinlan
All rights reserved. No part of this book may be reproduced, stored, or transmitted by any means—whether auditory, graphic, mechanical, or electronic—without written permission of both publisher and author, except in the case of brief excerpts used in critical articles and reviews. Unauthorized reproduction of any part of this work is illegal and is punishable by law.

ISBN: 978-0-9991777-0-9 (Paperback)

Printed in the U.S.A.

Book Design by DesignForBooks.com

# Contents

Introduction   v

1. The Daniel Fast   1
2. Fasting Is Not about You   5
3. Empowerment within You for This Time   11
4. Releasing Hidden Revelation   13
5. Finding a Place to Hear Clearly   19
6. The Preparation Time of Our Offering   23
7. The Length of a Fast Day   27
8. Your Day of Fasting   31
9. The Sabbath Day   37
10. The Strangers in the Atmosphere   39
11. The Health Benefits   43
12. Fasting Hygiene Information   45
13. Prayer during Fasting   47

# Introduction

The objective of *A Guide to Christian Prayer and Fasting* is to challenge readers to consider a higher level of presenting their bodies to God. The offering of giving themselves is the believer's greatest personal offering they can present to the Lord. The purpose of *A Guide to Christian Prayer and Fasting* is to share with the reader a fresh, exciting perception of commitment to Christ. The desire of the Christian today should be to draw nearer to God, in his or her relationship with Christ. The greatest personal offering that a person can give to God is him- or herself. Jesus wants to do his will in the life of the believer; our body is his temple for him to work in. God loved the world so much that he gave humanity his only begotten son so that the world might have life. With that being the case, what can we give in return to show our gratitude for such a gift? The answer is us. All God has ever wanted from man since the creation of Adam is fellowship and obedience. For man to keep God's commandments is the ultimate offering that Adam could render. God wanted Adam to yield to him by keeping his commandments.

After disobeying God's commandment, for the first time Adam attempted to hide from God's voice in the garden. He and Eve had made fig leaves to hide what they perceived to be shameful: their nakedness. The eating of the tree of knowledge of good and evil resulted in their consciousness of their nakedness and fear to hide from God in the garden, their first taste of disobedience. Afterward, God made both Adam and Eve coats of skins. It was never God's desire for them to be ashamed of their nakedness. If they had obeyed God, their nakedness would never have been an issue. Obeying God would have been the greatest gift that they could have given.

Historically, obedience has been the greatest gift man has given to God. God has sought obedience generation after generation. Jesus' will to keep his father's commandments pleased God.

The religious denominations of today have shaped current teaching by reviewing customs and doctrinal teachings of the Old Testament. This is wonderful because one of the customs is fasting. The apostle Paul explains that the Old Testament scriptures were given to us for our learning and benefit:

> For even Christ pleased not himself; but, as it is written, The reproaches of them that reproached thee fell on me. For whatsoever things were written aforetime were written for our learning, that we through patience and comfort of the scriptures might have hope. (Rom 15:3–4 KJV)

Here, Paul helps us to understand what was written in Isaiah 58 concerning the objective and benefits of fasting. Fasting develops and builds a personal relationship with God.

Important: Fasting is not mandatory—it is to be done voluntarily. It is the personal choice of the believer. It is the ultimate sacrifice that the believer can render to the Lord. Fasting is the gift of gifts and the highest form of worship. What can we offer to the Lord that really belongs to us? All the silver and gold belongs to him, so all I really have to give is me. When I fast, I am saying, "Lord, I give you me for your use, to give you glory in my body on the earth." When we examine the lives and habits of the patriarchs, we can see those who fasted for direction, favor, gratitude, and gain.

> *Fasting is not mandatory—it is to be done voluntarily.*

> Then all the children of Israel, and all the people, went up, and came unto the house of God, and wept, and sat there before the Lord, and fasted that day until even, and offered burnt offerings and peace offerings before the Lord. (Jgs 20:26 KJV)

# The Daniel Fast

The real benefit of fasting is that the person fasting causes his or her body to become submissive allowing the body to become a vessel for the will of the Lord to operate within giving him glory. I understand that fasting the way they did in the Bible is not acceptable for believers in this day and age. The flesh is opposed to the personal discomfort it brings. So today's believers modify fasting so that it will be more appealing. For example, study the "Daniel fast." We must realize it was Daniel's choice not to induce defilement by eating anything from the king's selected menu. Daniel asked the chief official for permission not to defile himself. As a Hebrew, Daniel was forbidden to eat the king's menu, so God caused the official to show favor and sympathy to Daniel. But the official told Daniel, "I am afraid of my lord the king, who has assigned your food and drink." The official explained to Daniel that the king would have his head if the health of Daniel and the other servants decayed.

Daniel then said to the guard who was appointed over them, "Please test your servants for ten days: Give us nothing but vegetables to eat and water to drink. Then compare our appearance with that of the young men who eat the royal food, and treat your servants in accordance with what you see." The outcome after ten days of eating nothing but vegetables and drinking water; Daniel and the three Hebrew boys appearance was more radiant than the others. (Daniel 1:11–15)

> *Prayer and fasting are desired to create an opportunity to deny the flesh while building one's faith . . .*

The Daniel fast involves eating only fruits and vegetables for a certain amount of time and abstaining from meat products. Some people use the Daniel fast as a dieting method. Because Daniel was a prisoner in captivity, he deviated from the instructions of Isaiah 58. Some people use the Daniel fast instead of fasting from food entirely, as Isaiah instructs. The Bible does not command believers to observe the Daniel fast. In fact, the only place where fasting is outlined in the Bible is in the book of Isaiah.

Prayer and fasting are desired to create an opportunity to deny the flesh while building one's faith; fasting will prove to be uncomfortable to the flesh. Isaiah clearly maps out the attitude we should have as we begin fasting. I have selected the New King James Version here because of its simplicity and clarity on this subject.

# Fasting Is Not about You

> Indeed you fast for strife and debate, And to strike with the fist of wickedness. You will not fast as you do this day, To make your voice heard on high. Is it a fast that I have chosen, A day for a man to afflict his soul? Is it to bow down his head like a bulrush, And to spread out sackcloth and ashes? Would you call this a fast, And an acceptable day to the Lord? (Is 58:4–5 NKJV)

Isaiah is instructed in chapter 58, verses 1–3, to proclaim to the people—with a shout and with boldness—what is wrong in their lives and to show them their sins. God tells Isaiah to inform them that they are so busy about nothing and that they seem to be busy, busy, busy, yet it's all about nothing. Remember, Jesus said the same to a group in the book of Matthew:

> Many will say to me in that day, Lord, Lord, have we not prophesied in thy name? and in thy name have cast out devils? and in thy name done many wonderful works? And then will I profess unto them, I never knew you: depart from me, ye that work iniquity. (Mt 7:22–23 KJV)

How are we so busy doing things that are not important to the objective of the kingdom of God? Where are the prophets, apostles, evangelists, pastors, and teachers who have the awesome assignment of instructing God's people in these last days? We are so busy giving things to the Lord that he didn't ask us to give. We give him church attendance, and that's good. We give him tithes and offerings, and that's also good. But what about a body that Jesus can work in? What about a life that is given so fully to the Lord that all people can see is Jesus? The apostle Paul teaches us about this:

> I am crucified with Christ: nevertheless I live; yet not I, but Christ liveth in me: and the life which I now live in the flesh I live by the faith of the Son of God, who loved me, and gave himself for me. (Gal 2:20 KJV)

> By the grace of God I am what I am: and his grace which was bestowed upon me was not in vain; but I labored more abundantly than they all: yet not I, but the grace of God which was with me. (1 Cor 15:10 KJV)

The book of Revelation must be given divine attention as we are now living in the end times to which it speaks. God is speaking expressly in these last days to his people through his Spirit:

> Now the Spirit speaketh expressly, that in the latter times some shall depart from the faith, giving heed to seducing spirits, and doctrines of devils. (1 Tm 4:1 KJV)

> He that hath an ear let him hear what the Spirit saith unto the churches. (Rv 3:6 KJV)

Fasting will give us a keener ear to hear what God is really saying to each of us individually through his Spirit. Both John, the Beloved Apostle, and the prophet Isaiah had the same assignments in different dispensations of time. Both of them declared to the people where they were wrong and instructed them to make changes.

In Isaiah 58, God instructs Isaiah to explain why he does not accept the fasting his people are rendering to him: "Well, here's why: 'The bottom line' on your 'fast days' is profit. You drive your employees much too hard. You fast, but at the same time you bicker and fight. You fast, but you swing a mean fist. The kind of fasting you do won't get your prayers off the ground. Do you think this is the kind of fast day I'm after: a day to show off humility? To put on a pious long face and parade around solemnly in black? Do you call that fasting, a fast day that I, God, would like?"

This fast was unacceptable because it was all about them, and they thought it would bring personal benefit. They used the day to showcase the perception that they were humble. They exalted themselves in their own minds while comparing themselves to others, wanting to appear spiritual. They didn't understand that prayer and fasting were to prepare them to be used by the Lord, for his purpose and glory on the earth. God had Isaiah declare to them what he required. This is why Jesus fasted—to offer to his father what he required. This is why we should fast—to present to God what he desires:

> *... prayer and fasting were to prepare them to be used by the Lord, for his purpose and glory on the earth.*

"This is the kind of fast day I'm after: to break the chains of injustice, get rid of exploitation in the workplace, free the oppressed, cancel debts. What I'm interested in seeing you do is: sharing your food with the hungry, inviting the homeless poor into your homes, putting clothes on the shivering ill-clad, being available to your own families. Do this and the lights will turn on, and your lives will turn around at once. Your righteousness will pave your way. The God of glory will secure your passage. Then when you pray, God will answer" (Is 58:6–9).

This is what God yearns for, and why; because fasting is not meant to be for us—it is so that God can touch the lives of others through us. God wants to touch humankind by working in our lives using our hands, our feet, our love, and our hearts, but it is really him working in us. So all the wonderful works that we do are not us; they are Jesus working in us by his Spirit. That is why the greatest gift that we can offer to the Lord is our bodies for him to work through. This is why Jesus was led into the wilderness: he was preparing himself to destroy the flesh, so he could allow the work that the father wanted, to work in him, in the flesh, on the earth.

Let's look at the objective, purpose, and end result that God was developing in the believer through the understanding of fasting. God wanted his people to understand that fasting would allow his will to operate by his Spirit in us, on the earth. He also wanted them to understand the benefits that would come upon us. These benefits will rest upon all who will allow him to perform his will in them. As we review Isaiah and look at the life of Jesus after the wilderness experience, we see why and when Jesus called upon the father, and the father answered him:

> You'll call out for help and I'll say, "Here I am" (Is 58:9)

> If you get rid of unfair practices, quit blaming victims, quit gossiping about other people's sins, If you are generous with the hungry and start giving of yourselves to the down-and-out, Your lives will begin to glow in the darkness with the glory of God, your darkened lives will be consumed in sunlight of the Lord. I will always show you where to go. (Is 58:9–11 MSG)

> I'll give you a full life in the emptiest of places—firm muscles, strong bones. You'll be like a well-watered garden, a gurgling spring that never runs dry. You'll use the old rubble of past lives to build a new,

rebuild the foundations from out of your past. You'll be known as those who can fix anything, restore old ruins, rebuild and renovate, make the community livable again. (Is 58:11–12 MSG)

If you watch your step on the Sabbath and don't use my holy day for personal advantage, If you treat the Sabbath as a day of joy, God's holy day as a celebration, If you honor it by refusing "business as usual," making money, running here and there—Then you'll be free to enjoy God! Oh, I'll make you ride high and soar above it all. I'll make you feast on the inheritance of your ancestor Jacob. (Is 58:13–14 MSG)

Yes! God says so!

When a child of God discovers that the greatest gift is presenting his or her body as a living sacrifice, he or she will discover the key that unlocks tremendous joy in the heart of God. The Lord desires one gift from every child born into the kingdom. That gift is to render him- or herself unto him. Hopefully, the reader will realize that surrendering to Jesus is the only battle fought in the Christian's walk that will make a difference.

# Empowerment within You for This Time

We have power to yield our bodies to the power of Christ, which works within us. We are not just abstaining from food; we are placing our rebellious, fleshly bodies and personal wills in subjection to the service of Christ. We want to give ourselves to God as living sacrifices for his pleasure and his use on the earth.

The more time we can spend with the Lord fasting, the better it will be for us. This quality time with the Lord honors him. This is the day that we are offering ourselves unto the Lord. This time should be spent reading the Word and meditating. Reading aloud during this time is powerful because as you declare God's word into the atmosphere, things will happen. This time is when you declare into the atmosphere that you are Christ's vessel for his service. Power manifests by the spoken word!

> That ye present your bodies a living sacrifice, holy, acceptable unto God, which is your reasonable service. And be not conformed to this world: but be ye transformed by the renewing of your mind, that ye may prove what is that good, and acceptable, and perfect, will of God. (Rom 12:1–2 KJV)

> Wherefore when he cometh into the world, he saith, Sacrifice and offering thou wouldest not, but a body hast thou prepared me. (Heb 10:5)

The Lord desires that we present ourselves as living sacrfice to him. When we totally surrender our physical bodies, which are his temple (mind, soul, and spirit), to Christ, he gets glory on the earth. If we do this, he is able to keep us. Jesus is able to keep our minds and souls if we place them into his hands:

> For the which cause I also suffer these things: nevertheless I am not ashamed: for I know whom I have believed, and am persuaded that he is able to keep that which I have committed unto him against that day. (2 Tm 1:12 KJV)

# Releasing Hidden Revelation

Often we read the Word of God without consideration of hidden revelation in the text. We fail to realize revelation is revealed by the Spirit. Often we depend on our surface human understanding for spiritual information. We must remember that God, the author of the word, wrote the word as he moved upon men by his Spirit:

> For the prophecy came not in old time by the will of man: but holy men of God spake as they were moved by the Holy Ghost. (2 Pt 1:21 KJV)

> All scripture is given by inspiration of God, and is profitable for doctrine, for reproof, for correction, for instruction in righteousness: That the

> man of God may be perfect, thoroughly furnished unto all good works. (2 Tm 3:16–17 KJV)

Just as the Spirit of God moved holy men to write the necessary scriptures for doctrine, reproof, and correction—that the people of God might be furnished in righteousness—God also, by his Spirit, reveals teachings to his people that they might be perfect and have good works. Therefore, the Spirit of God, in his people, was the author and inspiration of the writing of the prophets. This being so, God knows what he meant to say in the scriptures and to whom he wanted the understanding of the revelations to be revealed. He has chosen to reveal the hidden things of the scriptures to his people by his Spirit. One of the reasons for hiding divine revelations in the scriptures is that at an appointed time in the past, present, and future, God could and can reveal information necessary to the people of those times. In various dispensations of time, spiritual information and revelation are pertinent to one generation or people—yet not to everyone. This has occurred and does occur generation after generation.

> But we speak the wisdom of God in a mystery, even the hidden wisdom, which God ordained before the world unto our glory: Which none of the princes of this world knew: for had they known it, they would not have crucified the Lord of glory. (1 Cor 2:7–8 KJV)

There is a carnal understanding, but there is also a spiritual understanding, which is revelation. God, by his Spirit, makes known information from the Word of God. God has chosen to hide his divine wisdom, understanding, and revelation of the scriptures from the wisdom of men. Here is a perfect example of kingdom information or spiritual understanding (revelation) in the Word of God being hidden from the wisdom of men.

As it is written:

> Eye hath not seen, nor ear heard, neither have entered into the heart of man, the things which God hath prepared for them that love him. But God hath revealed them unto us by his Spirit: for the Spirit searcheth all things, yea, the deep things of God. For what man knoweth the things of a man, save the spirit of man which is in him? even so the things of God knoweth no man, but the Spirit of God. Now we have received, not the spirit of the world, but the spirit which is of God; that we might know the things that are freely given to us of God. Which things also we speak, not in the words which man's wisdom teacheth, but which the Holy Ghost teacheth; comparing spiritual things with spiritual things. (1 Cor 2:9–13 KJV)

The Word became flesh and dwelled among us, and we beheld the glory of the father working in the son. Jesus declared on several occasions what his assignment on the earth was: "I come to do the will of my father."

> ... though ye believe not me, believe the works: that ye may know, and believe, that the Father is in me, and I in him. (Jn 10:38 NIV)

Jesus was the greatest gift to all humanity. He was the manifestation of the Word in the flesh, the son God wanted on the earth. Then Jesus declares,

> Verily, verily, I say unto you, He that believeth on me, the works that I do shall he do also; and greater works than these shall he do; because I go unto my Father. (Jn 14:12)

Fasting will allow our spiritual ears to hear clearly the Spirit of God, which is within us. God operates his will through his Spirit from the inside of the believer, without outside interference. The only resistance to the Word of God operating in the believer is the operation of the lust of the flesh, the lust of the eye, or the pride of life.

> The Comforter, which is the Holy Ghost, whom the Father will send in my name, he shall teach you all things, and bring all things to your remembrance, whatsoever I have said unto you. (Jn 14:26)

These are a few scripture references pertaining to the subject of the Spirit of God speaking directly to the child of God to give him or her direction concerning things taught:

But this shall be the covenant that I will make with the house of Israel; After those days, saith the Lord, I will put my law in their inward parts, and write it in their hearts; and will be their God, and they shall be my people. And they shall teach no more every man his neighbour, and every man his brother, saying, Know the Lord: for they shall all know me, from the least of them unto the greatest of them, saith the Lord; for I will forgive their iniquity, and I will remember their sin no more. (Jer 31:33–34 KJV)

Howbeit when he, the Spirit of truth, is come, he will guide you into all truth: for he shall not speak of himself; but whatsoever he shall hear, that shall he speak: and he will shew you things to come. He shall glorify me: for he shall receive of mine, and shall shew it unto you. (Jn 16:13–14 KJV)

That the God of our Lord Jesus Christ, the Father of glory, may give unto you the spirit of wisdom and revelation in the knowledge of him: The eyes of your understanding being enlightened; that ye may know what is the hope of his calling, and what the riches of the glory of his inheritance in the saints. (Eph 1:17–18 KJV)

These things have I written unto you concerning them that seduce you. But the anointing which ye have received of him abideth in you, and ye need not that any man teach you: but as the same anointing teacheth you of all things, and is truth, and is no lie, and even as it hath taught you, ye shall abide in him. (1 Jn 2:26–27 KJV)

He that hath an ear, let him hear what the Spirit saith unto the churches; He that overcometh shall not be hurt of the second death. (Rv 2:11 KJV)

# Finding a Place to Hear Clearly

Finding a quiet, still, calm place to hear the voice of God is crucial. In this time of cell phones, etc., it can be tremendously challenging to find a place to hear the voice of the Lord clearly, without interruption. Identifying the voice of God takes time; we have to distinguish God's voice from the many voices we hear daily. Understand that your flesh is one of the voices that wants your attention during your search for a place. Hearing God and knowing that it is his voice are the most important elements in developing a relationship of trust with God. The challenge is that, in the course of a day, there are many voices trying to get our attention in conjunction with the seductive demonic activity in the atmosphere. In spite of and in the midst of all these voices trying to get our attention daily, God speaks to us.

Here is an exercise: Get up early in the morning and sit in a quiet place. Just be still before the Lord. Sit for about thirty to forty minutes. Pay attention to the thoughts that fill your mind—thoughts of suggestions to do something or go somewhere. Maybe there will be thoughts of the cares of the day or challenges to come. These voices will be amplified during this exercise, but know that they are speaking all the time. These voices are always suggesting something. We may not realize or even recognize them, but they are always speaking, trying to get our attention about something. And somewhere within the noise bombarding our mind, there is the voice of God speaking. This is why prayer, meditation, reading the Bible, and fasting are necessary in helping us to distinguish the voice of God from the seductive voices in the flesh and in the world. These worldly, seductive voices are trying to incite the lust of the eye, the lust of the flesh, and the pride of life that operate in our natural bodies.

The scriptures show Jesus being led by the Spirit into a quiet place away from the busyness of life. The wilderness is the quiet place to hear. Where can we go to isolate ourselves from the voices of the world to spend time with Jesus? The wilderness was not a strange destination for the great leaders of God; many became familiar with the voice of God

> *...prayer, meditation, reading the Bible, and fasting are necessary in helping us to distinguish the voice of God from the seductive voices in the flesh and in the world.*

and realized their callings. Moses, after killing the Egyptian, fled into the wilderness to a place called Midian for forty years. One day, Moses saw a bush that burned but was not consumed. God spoke to him from the bush, revealing to Moses his name and commanding him to return to Egypt and lead the Israelites out of bondage. Others who found themselves in isolated places—where they were separated from the cares of this life—include David before his kingship and Joseph after his rejection by his brothers. Joseph's brothers sold him, and he became a slave; then, he was imprisoned. Call it what you want, but you must admit that he was isolated, alone, and in a place of separation from the cares of life. And let's not forget Job, the apostle Paul, and the apostle John.

Let's look in the scriptures when Jesus was led by the Spirit into the wilderness. Wasn't he isolated and in a lonely place—a place of separation from the cares of life?

> Then was Jesus led up of the Spirit into the wilderness to be tempted of the devil. And when he had fasted forty days and forty nights, he was afterward an hungred. (Mt 4:1–2 KJV)

God led Jesus into the wilderness in preparation for his earthly assignment. The Word made manifest in the flesh so Jesus would have to deal with the rebellion of the flesh also. So isolation and separation would create the environment necessary to test the flesh as well as the willingness of Jesus to offer himself to his father to do his father's will. The wilderness would bring the temptation from within and without. His flesh would become hungry, and the tempter, the devil, would try to seduce him into giving in to the will of the flesh to eat rather than the will of the father to refrain from sustenance.

Isolation is the divine chemistry for manifesting real choices within a person. We, as the children of God, need to be (not successfully, of course) toward unfaithfulness in our commitment to God. We as believers must understand that this formula works every time when we are serious about yielding our bodies as instruments of God rather than to the lustful drives of the flesh. The world needs to see that we have yielded our bodies, our lives, and our lifestyles to God, for his glory.

# The Preparation Time of Our Offering

Our greatest sacrifice will be the shutting down of our day to spend time with Jesus. This shutting down from the world around us to spend time for our preparation for the Lord's use is the greatest offering we as believers can give to the Lord. One of the major challenges in the kingdom today is that people do not have quality, uninterrupted time to spend with God. Life demands every minute available in our day. There is not enough time in our day to get to every assignment we have planned. Therefore, remember yesterday's unfinished business will always attempt to imposes itself upon the new day. This is why there is never enough time to do all the things we feel we should do.

In the book of Haggai, God warns his people about having time for their business but no time for the things he is concerned about. He warns them, saying, "Consider your ways":

> Now therefore thus saith the LORD of hosts; Consider your ways. Ye have sown much, and bring in little; ye eat, but ye have not enough; ye drink, but ye are not filled with drink; ye clothe you, but there is none warm; and he that earneth wages earneth wages to put it into a bag with holes. Thus saith the LORD of hosts; Consider your ways. (Hg 1:5–7 KJV)

This is the same warning that the Spirit echoes in the ears of believers today. The apostle John gives the people of God the same warning in Revelation from the island of Patmos. Consider your ways! We have time for everything we desire to do, yet we have no time to give to the Lord what he desires—no time for the one who provides for our every need. We have become so busy about our affairs that we give no real consideration to what Jesus wants to have done in our lives as well as on the earth.

Remember the parable of the king's supper? This is another example recorded in the Word of God concerning time for God's issues. The master prepared a supper and gave those who were to be invited advanced notice. When the supper was ready and the master called, they were too busy with the concerns of life, and all requested to be excused.

This is the mind-set of Christians today: "I don't have time." Life has consumed our time; we have forgotten that Jesus is the giver of life, and Jesus can't even get real time with us. We want Jesus to bless us with his life and its benefits, yet we have no quality time to meet with him.

> When one of them that sat at meat with him heard these things, he said unto him, Blessed is he that shall eat bread in the kingdom of God. Then said he unto him, A certain man made a great supper, and bade many: And sent his servant at supper time to say to them that were bidden, Come; for all things are now ready. And they all with one consent began to make excuse. The first said unto him, I have bought a piece of ground, and I must needs go and see it: I pray thee have me excused. And another said, I have bought five yoke of oxen, and I go to prove them: I pray thee have me excused. And another said, I have married a wife, and therefore I cannot come. (Luke 14:15–20 KJV)

Excuses are not lies; they are signs that there are matters of a greater personal importance. Remember, an excuse is just a reason not to be in attendance. It is given because the event is personally perceived to be of lesser importance. In the parable of the king's supper, those receiving prior invitations from the king were excited in the beginning. But time caused the supper to become a second priority. We should review this scripture first, because we must understand that time with God is extremely important and second, because what God really wants, once again, is his temple, which he died for. Jesus paid for us with his life on Calvary, we belong to him—we are not our own. This is the salvation deal we received as payment for our sins: kingdom benefits as children and eternal life. He receives our bodies as instruments for him to work the will of his father in us on the earth. He needs time with us to implement his plan in our lives on the earth.

> Ye are bought with a price: therefore glorify God in your body, and in your spirit, which are God's. (1 Cor 6:20 KJV)

> Ye are bought with a price; be not ye the servants of men. (1 Cor 7:23 KJV)

The question must be asked personally: What has priority in my life today that causes me to give an excuse not to yield totally to God? What has happened in my life that has changed my personal wanting to understand more, concerning the objective of this great plan of salvation? How has my love for the Lord and private time with him become unimportant? What things have my interest, my love, and my time? What excuse will I give for not seeking him every opportunity available to me to receive clarity concerning my part in his kingdom agenda?

*What has priority in my life today that causes me to give an excuse not to yield totally to God?*

# The Length of a Fast Day

I have found that believers are challenged to try what they perceive to be new things. I traveled the world; some are excited about divine revelation while others question the findings. In my early years of walking with Jesus, I was always inquisitive. I wanted to know why we did certain things certain ways. This was not to challenge anyone—I just wanted to know. So concerning fasting, I wanted to know how long an acceptable fast would be and how the men in the Bible did it.

The length of a biblical day is measured from the morning until the next morning. The length of a day was first measured in Genesis 1:5, which notes, "The evening and the morning were the first day."

For example, the Sabbath would begin on Friday evening between 4:30 A.M. and 5:00 A.M. Then the Sabbath would end on Sunday between 4:30 A.M. and 5:00 A.M. This is the time when the evening meets the morning. This is the part of the day when the transition and responsibilities take place between the moon and the sun.

The evening refers to the dawn of the night before the morning of the next day. This is better known to most people as about 4:30 A.M. The evening would be the part of the night or dawn just before the next morning. This is when the sun overtakes the night to rule a new day.

What difference does this timeline make? Keep in mind that God has a purpose in everything he does. The instructions are divinely calculated to bring about an expected outcome. The scriptures point out that there is a cycle in a day. The first day was recorded as the standard of the rest of the timeline in the remaining days of creation. Although the sun and the moon were not created until the fourth day, everything created in each prior day needed the cycle of both night and day. The book of Luke shows us this concept better using the Sabbath day: the phrase "when the Sabbath was past" points out the transition from the Sabbath day into the first day of the week, which is Sunday. They clearly came to the grave site of Jesus when it was still dark, or early Sunday morning:

> The first day of the week cometh Mary Magdalene early, when it was yet dark, unto the sepulchre, and seeth the stone taken away from the sepulcher. (John 20:1 KJV)

This scripture supports the fact that the end of the Sabbath (dawn) is early Sunday morning. Is it safe to conclude that a day is when the evening and the morning touch? Or when the night and the morning meet? This would actually be what the Bible calls dawn or early in the morning (while it is still dark). The timeline of a day is determined by the complete rotation of an evening meeting a morning.

# Your Day of Fasting

Understand that fasting and prayer go together. Fasting when coupled with prayer is not only the greatest personal gift that we can offer to the Lord it is also a faith builder: But ye, beloved, building up yourselves on your most holy faith, praying in the Holy Ghost (Jude 20 KJV). The more you overcome the struggles of the flesh, the more your faith will increase. Praying while fasting is how we learn what our personal struggles are and how to overcome them. Struggles in the flesh are a constant reality with every child of God. When we are fasting, our bodies want to shut down. It is during this time of fasting that we need to pay attention to the rebelling voices of our

*Struggles in the flesh are a constant reality with every child of God.*

flesh. These voices will express boredom, sleepiness, and an unwillingness to stay focused and on course. This is our opportunity to monitor these personal desires of our flesh as it wars against our will to please God. These are the moments in which we have to demand that our bodies obey both the will and good pleasure of God. These are the times of casting down the thoughts of things contrary to the will of God for us. This is when we are to rebuke these thoughts openly by speaking to them and verbally casting them out of our mind, replacing them with thoughts that are acceptable as children of God.

> For though we walk in the flesh, we do not war after the flesh: (For the weapons of our warfare are not carnal, but mighty through God to the pulling down of strong holds;) Casting down imaginations, and every high thing that exalteth itself against the knowledge of God, and bringing into captivity every thought to the obedience of Christ. (2 Cor 10:3–5 KJV)

*. . . victory begins in the mind.*

For many, this will be a new experience of overcoming the desires of their flesh. But this victory begins in the mind. During this time, you must exercise saying no to your flesh, reminding yourself that you are more than a conqueror. You are an overcomer, but this must first be established in your mind and then declared with your mouth. You will notice that the thoughts of your mind will constantly present a challenge to your commitment.

But the more you talk to the Lord during this time about what is happening within you, the easier it will be to overcome the challenge.

> Wherefore when he cometh into the world, he saith, Sacrifice and offering thou wouldest not, but a body hast thou prepared me: In burnt offerings and sacrifices for sin thou hast had no pleasure. Then said I, Lo, I come (in the volume of the book it is written of me,) to do thy will, O God. (Heb 10:5–7 KJV)

> I beseech you therefore, brethren, by the mercies of God, that ye present your bodies a living sacrifice, holy, acceptable unto God, which is your reasonable service. And be not conformed to this world: but be ye transformed by the renewing of your mind, that ye may prove what is that good, and acceptable, and perfect, will of God. (Rom 12:1–2 KJV)

When we give God our bodies as a living sacrifice, this is all he really wants from us. God wants us to give ourselves totally to him for his pleasure and his use to fulfill his kingdom agenda. While fasting, we come and stand before him while openly reevaluating our relationship with him. This kind of presentation takes time. We must be committed to spending

*While fasting, we come and stand before him while openly reevaluating our relationship with him.*

real quality time in his presence. We have the power and authority to consecrate our day to the Lord as a personal offering to our God.

As a pastor, I have learned that many new believers want to draw closer to the Lord, but they don't know how. When someone gives his or her life to Jesus, that person lacks an understanding of how to present him- or herself and what pleases God. This is not unusual. The apostle Paul confessed that he was willing to serve God but didn't know how:

> Now if I do that I would not, it is no more I that do it, but sin that dwelleth in me. I find then a law, that, when I would do good, evil is present with me. For I delight in the law of God after the inward man: But I see another law in my members, warring against the law of my mind, and bringing me into captivity to the law of sin which is in my members. O wretched man that I am! who shall deliver me from the body of this death? (Rom 7:20–24 KJV)

This lack of understanding provides great training for the new child of God. New believers need to be made aware that the struggles within them are normal. The new convert needs to understand that everyone in the body of Christ has a battle within his or her flesh daily—not always the same one, but there is one nonetheless. This is a necessary teaching so that we learn about repentance, confession, and the necessary request for help and guidance when encountering these battles. We need help from

Jesus by his Spirit. This is what the apostle Paul requested.

When we understand the need for God to help us, the times of prayer and worship become more intense. Our need for him becomes clearer. These times will be exciting and more enjoyable. Fasting correctly will result in a time of reinstatement and refreshing. There will be a personal commitment to God. You will enjoy a fresh start. You will discover that the glory of the Lord will rest upon you; he has promised that when you call, he will answer, "Here I am."

*Fasting correctly will result in a time of reinstatement and refreshing.*

> Then shall thy light break forth as the morning, and thine health shall spring forth speedily: and thy righteousness shall go before thee; the glory of the LORD shall be thy reward. Then shalt thou call, and the LORD shall answer; thou shalt cry, and he shall say, Here I am. If thou take away from the midst of thee the yoke, the putting forth of the finger, and speaking vanity; And if thou draw out thy soul to the hungry, and satisfy the afflicted soul; then shall thy light rise in obscurity, and thy darkness be as the noonday. (Is 58:8–10 NIV)

There are requirements for this fast to have the results promised in the latter parts of Isaiah 58. One of them is that we only fast on the days when we are not working. It is imperative to be able to give our day to the Lord. One of the reasons God rejected Israel's day of fasting was that during the day, they found time for their personal pleasures. We cannot give God anything that is not ours to give. When our employers hired us, they bought our time for the day, and they expect us to give it totally to them for those hours in which they are paying.

> *We cannot give God anything that is not ours to give.*

Many may say, "I only have two days off per week to take care of my personal business." This is why those days are special; they become one of the most valuable parts of your sacrifice. This is what makes the day a real offering to the Lord. They are your days, and this is your time. David declared, "I will not offer unto the Lord that which cost me nothing" (2 Sm 24:24).

What better fasting day to give to the Lord for an offering than your own time and your day off? What better sacrifice to offer to the Lord during your time than yourself?

# The Sabbath Day

There is much controversy concerning the subject of the Sabbath as the time of rest. The fasting day(s) you select could include your day of worship (Sunday, or for other religious groups, Saturday). You can privately make your commitment to God while gathering in services with the body of believers for worship while using the day as your fast day. It was a custom for the Israelites to combine fasting on the day of rest (the Sabbath) with meeting in the temple for worship. There were other days of the week also used for both fasting and worship. These times were not about them; they were times in which they gave thanks to the Lord for his goodness to his people.

> Wherefore have we fasted, say they, and thou seest not? Wherefore have we afflicted our soul,

and thou takest no knowledge? Behold, in the day of your fast ye find pleasure, and exact all your labours. (Is 58:3 KJV)

If thou turn away thy foot from the sabbath, from doing thy pleasure on my holy day; and call the sabbath a delight, the holy of the LORD, honourable; and shalt honour him, not doing thine own ways, nor finding thine own pleasure, nor speaking thine own words: Then shalt thou delight thyself in the LORD; and I will cause thee to ride upon the high places of the earth, and feed thee with the heritage of Jacob thy father: for the mouth of the LORD hath spoken it. (Is 58:13–14 NIV)

# The Strangers in the Atmosphere

Now in the twenty and fourth day of this month the children of Israel were assembled with fasting, and with sackclothes, and earth upon them. And the seed of Israel separated themselves from all strangers, and stood and confessed their sins, and the iniquities of their fathers. (Neh 9:1–2 KJV)

In the Old Testament, the strangers referred to the Gentiles in the land. These were the ones who had no relationship with the God of the Israelites. These were not heirs to the covenants and promises of Abraham. They did not adhere to the commandments of God or the voice of his prophets. These are also referred to in the scriptures as the mixed multitude.

This group identified as strangers included nations who were not the descendants of Abraham. These nations continued to live as they pleased and celebrated the lusts of their flesh. They refused to have their personal pleasures interrupted. These strangers were the ones responsible for influencing the thinking of the children of God, causing many to embrace their pagan ideas. The acceptance of these pagan ideas left the children of Israel deaf of hearing and rebellious toward the commandments of God. God's people participated with the strangers who served other gods, caused Israel to turn against God's commandments, and caused Israel's hearts to become hardened. Their ears could not hear the voice of God. Israel forgot the original warning of God given to them by Joshua in Deuteronomy, when the Lord warned them of fellowshipping with strangers in the Promised Land:

> For they will turn away thy son from following me; that they may serve other gods: so will the anger of the LORD be kindled against you, and destroy thee suddenly. (Dt 7:4 KJV)

The likeness of these biblical strangers can be found today around us. One of the areas often undetected is the immoral transmission of information through television, radio, newspapers, and the Internet. Many people are addicted to various programs and games; every day, they spend hours being entertained. These groups would be referred to today as the strangers. They often steal God's time with his people. His people will not make the time to spend with the God of their salvation. No quality time for reading, meditating, and prayer. These are today's biblical strangers. They are the influencing forces and voices on the earth to which we give much of our time and attention.

Today, cell phones, television, social media, and the Internet are the main gathering places for information and entertainment. From the rising of the sun to the going down of the same, we are in front of some type of screen. Each family member watches the entertainment or information program of choice. Many are not mindful of the suggestive, influencing messages being transmitted. They are also unaware of their willingness to receive information that will later plague them. Many programs are the cause of the rebelliousness of children toward parents. These programs heighten the sexual appetites of our young men and women. The home has become the place where families eat, sleep, and isolate themselves on their PCs. It is the place where video games are played, television is watched, and the Internet is explored.

When we are fasting at home, if possible, we should shut off all electronic devices. This is how we personally draw ourselves from the distractions around us. This will help guard our minds from the things that entice their attention. There are many things that will interfere with the intended goal of offering yourself totally to the Lord.

# The Health Benefits

Consult your physician if you are under the care of one. I am not a physician, but I have benefited both spiritually and physically from fasting. One of the health benefits is an opportunity for the digestive system to rest. The body is not designed to digest food at night. Food gives us energy to perform during the day. Consequently, the most important meal of the day is breakfast. God has designed the body to complete the digestive process of breakfast during the daily activities. While resting, healing of the body will take place throught the night. It is during rest at night that rejuvenation, replenishing, and healing take place in the body. Diseases

> *. . . I have benefited both spiritually and physically from fasting.*

manifest in the digestive system and are transmitted through the blood. Many diseases gain a stronghold in our bodies because the consumption process never has an opportunity to complete the digestive cycle during the night. This is why many are challenged with high blood pressure, diabetes, weight gain, and even colon problems, to name a few. Therefore, eating large meals in the morning and light dinners before the setting of the sun will help the healing process of the digestive system complete its designed purpose. Changing our eating habits will aid in healing these wonderfully made bodies.

# Fasting Hygiene Information

For health and safety reasons, consume plenty of water on your fasting day. Water helps the body to discharge toxins collected in the body while fasting. If traveling, keep a toothbrush and some mouthwash handy to maintain fresh breath. Breath strips and breath drops are also good. Mints, candy, or gum should not be consumed as they are not good on an empty stomach; they will just become substitutes for food.

# Prayer during Fasting

I would like to share a prayer that will keep you focused during this time of fasting:

Lord, I give you this day to bless you. My soul bows, and I surrender all of me to you. I give you my will and my personal desires in exchange for yours. It is my desire to do your will. Here I am. Send me into your vineyard to perform your kingdom agenda.

Speak to me; I want to hear your voice and understand. Tell me what you need from me. It is my will to give you my body totally for your pleasure. My body is your temple. The members of my body are your instrments use them for your glory on the earth. I afflict my body with fasting, sacrificing it to you. I yield my mind for you to download your will and thoughts, that I may perform your will. I yield to you my heart to be sensitive to your voice and passion. My soul rejoices to perform your hope. Speak to me.

Help me understand your heart's desires. Use me for your glory. I want to be your praise. I know it is your will to rest your glory upon me as your ambassador on the earth. I know it is your desire to shine through in my life that he might see you in me.

I understand my life is how you win souls. Lord, let them see you manifested in my life. Teach me how to walk before men. Teach me how to speak life and hope into the lives of men. Increase my passion and love for all souls. Move me by your spirit; I am yours. Speak to me; I want to hear. Teach me; I want to learn. Use me; I want your joy and pleasure to be full. In the name of Jesus!

> *Lord, let them see you manifested in my life.*

www.ingramcontent.com/pod-product-compliance
Lightning Source LLC
Chambersburg PA
CBHW021136300426
44113CB00006B/455